Tree

Tree

Poems by Paula Day
with photography by Val Corbett

To Priscilla
with best wishes.
Paula Day
October 2013

Published by Daylight

Acknowledgements

Janni Howker's Kendal nature poetry workshop was the
seed-bed for these poems. I am grateful to all the group
members for their support and feedback, and especially to
Alison Easton and Janni herself, who read the manuscript
and gave me good advice when I couldn't see the
wood for the trees.

Val Corbett's gorgeous photographs illuminate the book.
My thanks to her for her patience and perseverance,
especially in quest of the right kind of dead tree!

My mother's eye for plant form, my father's feel for wood,
are always in my mind. They showed me how to look,
and delight in what I see.

Copyright © Daylight 2013
Poems and text copyright © Paula Day 2013
Photographs copyright © Val Corbett 2013

Designed by Zinco Design Solutions
Printed in Cumbria on 100% recycled paper by Absolute Digital Print
Published by Daylight
ISBN 978-0-9576504-0-4

www.treebydaylight.co.uk

Contents

Part Three: Family Tree

Introduction

In trees, the greatest of all plants, we humans seem to meet our match. Like us, they have evolved to stand upright on the earth. Like us, they are unique individuals, each with a distinctive character. They too have long lives. We thrive in similar places.

The poems in the first part of this book, *Touch Wood*, trace a lifetime of relationships with trees. As a baby I gazed up at the street tree outside the window of our London house. In later childhood I ran wild in the woods at our cottage in West Sussex, the most forested of all English counties, while my father collected and sawed logs for the fire, and my mother planted a garden. Then as an adult I settled in Cumbria. The sheep-grazed northern hills are much less densely wooded, but trees standing alone on open ground often have great presence. Our land here includes orchard, wood pasture, and a strip of ancient enclosed woodland, so we live alongside the trees which provide us with fruit, beanpoles and firewood. I have learned about coppicing and pollarding, felling and planting, woodland history and wildlife, through satisfying hands-on work with trees.

The more closely I look and listen, the more fascinating I find these giant organisms which stand among us, often scarcely noticed. Different trees catch my attention as they unfold through the seasons. I imagined what I would say to each of the twenty-one species which grow within a mile of my home, or what they would say about themselves, if they could talk. The poems in *A Year of Tree*

Riddles invite you to play a guessing-game – which tree is speaking? Or you might want to peek at the *Answers*, to find the common name (the titles are the botanical ones) and some of the facts behind the poems.

Finally, the *Family Tree* poems explore the experience of bereavement and inheritance, in the wake of losing my parents. Aged trees offer a direct living connection with our ancestors. And, with their annual renewals, their regenerations, their sheer will to grow, trees everywhere affirm life.

When I first moved north my neighbour was Val Corbett, now an acclaimed photographer, whose magnificent books and national magazine pieces have opened people's eyes to the Cumbrian landscape. I asked her to collaborate, and she responded with characteristic gusto. Making this book with her has been a delight.

Paula Day

Tree Book

Feel the coolness overhead. With ape arms
swing up the ladder of branches. Hand myself
mouthfuls of juicy leaves and fruits.

Fret sticks together. Feed the spark
dry twigs. Savour the warmth,
bright in the dark.

Light up my mind. Look up
at the long-legged green creature whispering.
Wonder. How was it made?

With fire charcoal scratch branching
marks. Score runes. Make words,
make a 'tree', see,

entirely made of words! And another!
Make a whole wood of words!
A whole new world!

Into the forest send a monster machine
to bite off a pine, chew it up and
spit it out, press it thin

as peeled birch bark, chop it into pieces
flat as leaves, stamp them with words.
Stack up the leaves a hundred or so deep,

thick and weighty as a small wooden plank
I can pick up in my hands, like a juicy fruit,
like a stick to make a spark. Call it 'Tree'.

Part One
Touch Wood

First Love

I think I was imprinted on a London plane.
From my cot, I'd stare
up at the sky-riding twig kite,
turkeycock, Indian brave, Paul Klee lady-in-a-hat
bounding and bucking,
seed-balls bobbing, bouncing like yo-yos,
scraping and scribbling and scratching
at itself, yet always there.

Titania woke, and saw Bottom; I, a tree.
And in autumn now I glory
in sulphur, ochre, russet, tawny;
touch of fabric ribbed or satin,
napped or gloss or felt, on expectant skin;
slipping off, sliding, shedding, showing
the strange, distinctive, closely-studied,
beloved line and lean of limb and limb.

Maylight

Maylight
feeding frenzy:
leaf shoals swarm
out of twigs,
swimming light,
flicking this way and that,
to suck sun.
Sycamore holds out
a workhouse's worth of
flimsy paper plates
wanting MORE.
Caterpillars munch, inch
towards tit's quick peck.
Sparrowhawk sweeps all.

Big city buzz
in the twenty-four-hour woods:
skyscraper heights
of the oaks hum with night-
life, blackbird's song
revving up before dawn,
fluorescent glare
follows badger down her lair,
pulls fox cubs out
to roister about,
yells at the woman
who wants to sleep on
into daylight:
'Maylight!'

Neighbours

Not starting out before sunset
to squat, circumspectly stationed
downwind the sett, chilled

stiff, waiting
at last to catch a glimpse
of a striped mask far off

before dark reclaims it. Not,
in fact, hoping at all, not
expecting anything, only

wandering footsoft in the breathless evening,
slowing into kinship with tall trunks alongside,
allowing the light

to fail, myself
to fade, open-
eyed

to you,
out of another world
hurrying down through tussocks towards me

regardless. Snuffing grubbing working
our track's wide floor, your feeding ground,
six feet away

from mine. Joined
by you others born out of the hill,
small ones lunging and chasing

as if this place was all yours.
And your ash-grey hulk hauling easy up the wall,
treading familiar topstones over

into the many-pathed wood.
Then they were gone. In darkness
I went home.

Seven Days on the South Downs Way

Where I live, the mountains are measured in metres.
But these hills I first walked unroll in miles,
ten, twenty, the whole hundred of the South Downs Way.
At the start Seven Sisters form a rampart against the sea.
The Devil tried to dig a Dyke right through to flood the Weald
where northern scarps scoop up to a grassy crest
that bounds along the whole length of Sussex.

Downs swell up and sweep,
rugged with black-and-white yew and ash,
full colour plantations of beech,
or bare in raked chalk-dusted hectares
wisping green with winter wheat,
cropping up flints like builders' rubble,
like broken bits of mangel-wurzel.

The calcareous earth holds also the bones
of a hundred generations: Iron Age barrows
at Chanctonbury Ring, Firle Beacon,
surviving still in summit sun;
under the dark north face, Didling and Buriton's
churches squat among mossy gravestones;
East Meon's woodland burial ground, mounds freshly heaped.

And all along I see through the living
eyes of the loving dead:
Paul Nash by the track painting beeches;
Gilbert White glancing up from his Selborne study;
Virginia, Vanessa, and Duncan's open-
minded space down at Charleston;
Edward Thomas' long stride still pacing us on ahead.

Larks lift up a sky
that's banged down with clattering pheasants
and trundling range-rovers' rumble.
Ladybirds ride me for miles, on cuff or collar.
Labradors dragging their walkers run laughing by.
Palmer's sheep graze in peace; and in the half-moon sunset,
by the chalk-light path, thickets are twittering goodnight.

Their southern downland flora strangely
familiar, like cousins rarely seen:
between dogwood and bramble, the shocking pink
capsules of spindle; white campion's big soft stars;
maples' flutter of amber butterflies;
bryony's red swags; buckthorn's black beads;
the tarzan ropes of old man's beard, with his woolly blankets.

And the oval-, wrinkled-, matt-leaved shrub
tipped with next spring's parchment flower buds,
that accompanied me in the hedge, dumb, all the way
from Winchester to Beachy Head.
Till I consulted the botany book,
and we turned to each other and said
'Wayfaring Tree!'

How on Earth?

How on earth did they get up there?
Lodged in the very tops
of Uppark skyline's
long-boned limes,
great bushes, bunches, bundles,
green lit to brass by the low sun.

Were they hoisted up on pulleys?
Or did Brueghel's Babel builders
swarm up tiered ladders,
each humping a balloon
of white-berried sprigs,
bigger than himself,

the way they hauled the weathercock
(size of a wheelbarrow)
up Chichester cathedral steeple?
Where to this day it perches, surveying
all between Downs and France. Turns
its golden head, straight into the wind.

Bindwood, Lovestone

I introduced ivy to my house. Viridian flames
went licking slowly up, a lizard
of arrowy serpentine leaves
crawling close to the stone, a living mural,
a tall tree ironed flat
onto the wall, like a pressed flower.

A vertical garden. Branches swing out
shiny waterproof lobes, shelter chaffinch chicks
in their upstairs bed. Candelabra bearing
a November spring of starburst blossoms
buzzing with wings, a March harvest
of blueberries for blackbirds.

I am no great lover of the adhesive ivy
glueing itself in a dark, dowdy, dusty mass and mess
full of old birds' nests which ought to be cleared out.
As Milton rightly remarked, ivy is never sere. Sometimes
one wishes it were. One gets so bored (wrote Vita Sackville-West)
by its persistent stuffy evergreen.

When I was young we used to spend whole weekends
wrenching ivy off the great Sussex oaks. We'd sever
hirsute muscular trunks, lever
their cut ends away from the pillar they clung onto
with a trillion millipede arms.
You had to get a good grip, rip

the stiff plaits upwards like gigantic Velcro
showering bark dust in your eyes, unzip
twenty foot creepers to fall about the woods like collapsed ladders.
If fragile homes came littering down, we didn't notice,
or the lack of bats once it was gone.
Best clean out crawling creatures.

We were saving noble oaks
from the python stranglers
we believed sucked their sap.
It was the 1960s. Everywhere
people were pulling things down.

Damson Jam

Beat the thin
dishevelled tree
with sticks to cry
its leaden drops.

Stew blue eggs
to hatch amber yolks,
avalanche sugar
to soak up blood.

Stir and stir
till one by one
stones surface,
survivors in the foam.

Scoop them up
and tip them out,
build stone by stone
the seeping cairn.

Raise the boil
to rollick and roll,
erupt black bubblings,
fleeing scum,

satanic gouts
and incense swung,
till seething pitch
is dark and thick and runs.

Scald the ladle,
scald the funnel,
into scorched jars
dole and dribble.

Ten bay windows
gleam with garnet
velvet curtained
for the winter.

Sealed, preserved,
well done.

Feeding the Fire (Rebecca Oaks' Coppice Course)

When the wood-burning stove is craving food,
take your saw to the storehouse wood.
Mark the trees you decide to fell –
the sick, the skinny – in a coppicing cull.

Save that upright oak and that flourishing cherry
but put this sad ash out of its misery
of canker scabs and bleeding sap
and wilting leaves; for in the gap

left by its loss, its neighbours will grow
dense and robust. So seize the saw.
Work out which way you want it to fall
not to smash this fence or shatter that wall.

Make the first incision, stroking the skin,
rocking back and forth, till you're one-third in.
From higher up, carve down a notch
at a steepish angle to cut out a crotch.

Then go in for the kill on the other side
drawing the blade with a steady glide
towards the gaping hinge; there's a groaning creak;
a gasping crack; the sinews break

and the beast goes down, with a roaring crash
of breaking branches and scraping brash,
in its neighbours' embrace. Now we gather round
and drag the carcass right down to the ground.

Straighten our backs; stretch our arms;
admire our prize; suppress our qualms.
Pick up a billhook, with glancing blows
work up the trunk slicing off the boughs –

not cack-handed chops but an easy swing
parting limb from loin; that's good snedding.
Onto two lengths of twine laid out on the ground
toss the wands of brash, hold them down

with your foot, tie a slip-knot, bundle's bound.
Heave and handle it onto the heap
of kindling faggots. Then take a break.

Back from sandwiches, doggedly saw
through the thigh-thick trunk, making sure
you cut logs to the length your stove can stretch
its hungry jaws. If they'll squeeze through the hatch

they're short enough; don't make extra work.
Then set a log square on the chopping block.
Take up the sharp axe; plant your feet apart,
(so if you miss it's not them you'll cut).

Slide one hand down the shaft, swing it high,
bring it swingeing down so the two halves fly
apart like the skull of an Epic's slain.
Set another log up. Swing again.

Keep on swinging as the split logs fall
in a pile of spoil. When you've had your fill
chuck the booty into a barrow
and wheel it home for the stove to swallow.

But there's a catch: if you feed it raw
in reeking gobbets to a house-trained fire,
it will gag and sputter, its windpipe choke,
tarred, furred, coughing up smoke.

Logs must be patiently set aside,
cured, matured, lardered, dried
for at least a year. Meanwhile, you wait
to warm yourself, by an empty grate.

But you're not a monk; if you've no backlog
just suck instant fire through a flex and plug.
Yes, your stove will starve, but you can retreat
to the good old days of electric heat.

Ash Pollards

Pollards. Man-high knobbed bollards,
big as bulls, or moraine boulders.
Monsters with mad sticking-out hair.
Hunks. Gross contorted trunks
gawp and girn, bulge lips
round gaping scars.

One grips a fistful
of polypody fern, one a holly
or rowan sapling, growing
in its strong hold.
One's just a hulk
enclosing a dank hollow.

Undead stumps mark bounds
of Langdale fields, generations
farmed for fodder.
Poles are chopped off,
beasts browse the brash.
On stone hearths ash burns to ash.

You'd think the relentless crop
would weaken them, but no, they bunch
massive knuckles, gather gargantuan force
from vascular roots, throw up
a score of javelins,
pack a champion's punch.

The Ballad of Hackett's Wood

Old Farmer Hackett comes out of the hill
Whizz! Whizz! Zee-zee-whizz!
on a quad bike crusade to clean up the dale.
With a creak-crack-crash! Down they fall.

He rattles up the lane with his chainsaw cutter,
Whizz! Whizz! Zee-zee-whizz!
slices through the hedge like a knife through butter.
With a creak-crack-crash! Down they fall.

He's razed it down to sticks and stubble,
Whizz! Whizz! Zee-zee-whizz!
dumped on top subsoil and rubble.
With a creak-crack-crash! Down they fall.

Bird cherries blossom along the way.
Whizz! Whizz! Zee-zee-whizz!
They look too pretty. They must pay.
With a creak-crack-crash! Down they fall.

He rubs the stumps with spent sump oil,
Whizz! Whizz! Zee-zee-whizz!
and the brash blazes up like merry hell.
With a creak-crack-crash! Down they fall.

He ring-barks a beech so it dies on its feet.
Whizz! Whizz! Zee-zee-whizz!
Devil good job, that, nice and discreet.
With a creak-crack-crash! Down they fall.

He roars round the fields, chops and lops,
Whizz! Whizz! Zee-zee-whizz!
cuts the arms off the oaks so they're lollipops.
With a creak-crack-crash! Down they fall.

He heaps their limbs round them and burns them alive.
Whizz! Whizz! Zee-zee-whizz!
They'll be crippled and scarred even if they survive.
With a creak-crack-crash! Down they fall.

Out runs Patience in a sobbing bother.
Whizz! Whizz! Zee-zee-whizz!
'That oak was as dear as my sainted mother'.
With a creak-crack-crash! Down they fall.

Up jump the neighbours with a furious clamour,
Whizz! Whizz! Zee-zee-whizz!
'We're writing a letter to the Council Planner!'
With a creak-crack-crash! Down they fall.

He talks to the Planner, so polite.
Whizz! Whizz! Zee-zee-whizz!
She says 'he's quite reasonable, sweetness and light'.
With a creak-crack-crash! Down they fall.

He's caught poor Prudence down in the lane,
Whizz! Whizz! Zee-zee-whizz!
'I'll break your bloody neck if you try that again'.
With a creak-crack-crash! Down they fall.

He roves the land, beyond reach of the law,
Whizz! Whizz! Zee-zee-whizz!
till it's like a battlefield in the First World War.
With a creak-crack-crash! Down they fall.

Now Time has cut old Hackett down,
(whisper) *Whizz! Whizz! Zee-zee-whizz!*
laid him low from foot to crown.
(whisper) *With a creak-crack-crash! Down he falls.*

The neighbours, in memory of that farmer good,
(louder) *Whizz! Whizz! Zee-zee-whizz!*
have planted up an acre, named it 'Hackett's Wood'.
(shout) *AND THE BEECH-OAK-ASH SPRING UP TALL!*

Part Two

A Year of Tree Riddles

January

Crataegus monogyna

Crone, I squat, wizened by wind's whipping,
sheep's gnawing, frost biting me brittle.

Hair a tangle, skin ochre-blotched with lichen
or sprouting pale tufts, knobbed fossil fingers

gesticulate to my sisters flocking up the fell,
and huddled dense against the fences:

we'll grip fast this pasture, we'll crab, claw you, intruder,
we will last out the winter.

And, quick by March, I blush green before all others,
fringing with soft bristle, a boy's stubble.

May I marry, assuming his name,
yet, banned from the house – 'it would kill my mother' –

I traipse my dress dingy along the hedgerows,
smooching milk smuts of scent, making myself common.

By September I'm throwing a party.
Robed in stiffly beaded gown I proffer plenty,

waitress arms stacked to the elbows
with boojuns, asogs, arzy-garzies,
agags, hoppety-haws, the fieldfares' bread-and-cheese.

February

Betula pendula

Weedling (they say),
worth nothing,
gold shower over now,
yellow pennies all spent,
straggling along railway sidings
with your skinny siblings
all sizes, any number,
scraping a living.

Punk Goth,
face chalk
under purple-black
glossy shock,
slim trunk's
soft pink
masked by charcoal
tattoo scars.

Twiggy fascinator
sequined with drips
winking at long-tailed tits,
foxtrotting dapper gents,
kitted-to-match
in black tails, blush cravats,
to flirt, flitter, flick, turn another
trick-trick-trick.

Paperless poet
scoring Morse
on your own pearly skin,
pluming to a quill
to scratch spidery
graffiti, fine-
skeined inky lines,
on wintry sky.

Slip of a girl
springing up slag-heaps,
no man's spoil.
And on into the north
outrunning even the husky
fir and pine.
Silvery laughter
in the Arctic.

Alnus glutinosa

Where others would rot we're in our element –
flush, mire, carr, bog, or along
the beck's meanderings,

waterlogged to our swollen ankle boles.
Our mangrove roots consolidate
small islands. Fish flick

for sanctuary between our toes.
Our crust is crocodile scales.
Wine-dark in winter, we still cling

to carapaces, rusty screws of cones,
seeds long ago stream-sown,
and wriggle with larvae, purple till in spring

we dangle shrimp catkins.
Celandine and marsh marigold
beneath us shine unshaded. Our late leaves

glaze bottle green, untouched
by autumn colour. But if you cut us
our white flesh will bleed.

Salix caprea

Grey woods here and there
switch on lights for Easter.
Wave withy wands;
magic chicks!

Tiny yellow hedgehog!
Fuzzy lemon sherbet!
I run my lips along your downy muzzle,
touch your citrus-dipped brush-tip to my nose

to sniff the sucrose whiff.
I love you, little sexling!
Thready filaments twanged erect all over,
offering your pollen charge to every passer-bee!

April

Acer pseudoplatanus

Four-square out here on the moor, a weathered warrior,
massive trunk braced in flaking copper plates
verdigris with lichen, and moss-shaggy greaves,
flexing my branches, clashing my overlapped leaves,
I stand stalwart by the frontline fell farm,
facing the battery wind.

Now my shoulders are broad enough to bear
the old slight. That I'm not native, an alien, in spite
of five hundred years' service here.
That my leaves age ugly. Splotch
dirty black. Spit, and drop early
to smother and slime. The old hurt.

Now I take my proud place beside comrade ash,
with almost oaken gravitas.
Come feast with my family
as confetti-pink sepals are strewing down,
and we flirt blush vine-leaves,
dandle grape-bunch blossoms,
raise a flush of seedlings eager to forest the land.

Larix decidua

Ja, I'm from Switzerland. I know Wordsworth
didn't like me in his landscape,
and the dark pines scoff
'So you drop those blonde needles
like any nesh broadleaf,
when the year gets tough?'

But look, aren't I lovely,
I'm Greensleeves,
upswept branches stroking sky,
grassy bristles brushing
spring clean, feathering
wings as if to fly.

I make pink-topped cupcakes,
cornetto cones for summer.
In autumn I'll tint amber.
I'm an excellent au pair,
nannying new plantations.
In the end I'm useful timber.

Don't I earn my place here?

Ulmus glabra

Who am I, leaning
over the river gorge,
snaking my slim trunk, sinuous, bewitching,
pale green rosettes for corsage
on my fishbone sprays?

Soon I'll be leafing,
splaying long leaves.
Soon leaving. Like my upright cousin
whose towering corpse
stalked the fields.

May

Fraxinus excelsior

Tree, leafless in May,
skeleton at the feast, are you dead?
I'm sifting the sun,
fingering the light.
When will you leaf?
When the frosts are well past.

Why are your arms thrown up?
Are you in pain?
I lift, sway this way, swing away,
to the dance band wind.

What's that you're carrying,
whiskered and stiff?
Bunches of keys
to unlock barren earth.

And those cresting tufts,
flowers, female, male?
One year man, one year woman,
one year hermaphrodite and whole.

What will your leaves be like, tree?
Soft as cicely, fine as fern,
lime as spurge,
pinnate as rowan.

When will you drop them?
How will they fall?
At October's first frost
I'll unloose them all,
step out of the summer dress,
stand naked again.

Just four months to feed yourself!
How do you live?
Quick as I can,
never fear, never grieve.

You must grow small and slow.
None springs faster than me,
roots well fastened below,
wide crown scraping the sky.

And where do you grow?
Some rich garden enclosed?
On the high hard fell
out of limestone bones.

Prunus avium

Picture her fresh from the woods, poised beside a stone house,
Radiant in ruffled white for their May Day wedding.
Under her canopy blossom garden bridesmaids,
None so lovely. For a season she's docile green,
Until October re-ignites her wildness. A blazing beacon,
She shouts out summer's end to sisters scattered in the forest.

All the birds of the air dance among her boughs.
Visiting woodpeckers knock. Blue tits raise their blue tots
In her nestbox. Thrushes feast on her shiny red fruits, still
Unripe for humans. Treecreeper and nuthatch
Make their way up and down the shining road of her trunk.

Prunus padus

Picture them in the queue of an outgrown hedge, wearing
Racemes of creamy lace for the Whitsun Gala,
Unpretentious in their warm leaf cardigans.
Nicknamed old Heg, or Hags, or sour Heckberry,
Up and down the Dales these north country wives
Scent long June twilights with their almond fragrance.

Pity them in July, foliage quite stripped off,
Abused beyond recognition, crawling with caterpillars,
Draped, wound and bound in the ermine moth's mantle,
Ugly as sin, beautiful as a choking mink stole,
Shocking, a horror film along the home farm lane.

Fagus sylvatica

In the woods you meet a wall. A rootplate
wheel, twelve foot across, snapped
spokes poking out. Clutches of rock
cracked, like bones broken as a shattered
athlete's shocked sinews contract.

The underworld quaked. Worms' moist home
was ripped out into glare. Earth's surface
tilted, groundlings gazing up to heaven
tipped ninety degrees
to face bitter north-east.

Beyond this she lies. Flowing limbs
faintly glowing grey. Sprawled
headlong down the slope,
as if across a hospital bed.
Resting.   I remember

climbing through her, along her sliding
smooth mossed arms, when she stood
and I was young. Even then
her fine skin was inscribed
with scars and stretch-marks,

flesh tenderly creased and puckered
round offspring and navel.
Now her reclining trunk
grows a row of small upright trees.
Starting again from where she is.

How many more springs
she can greet, who knows.
From what little root still holds,
what living nerves and synapses still
connect, she's lit up green.

July

Quercus petraea x robur

Back from the south. Home. Earth stonier.
Light colder. Kirkbank shouldering higher
against Atlantic draughts. Sheep-eaten
bare, except where the guardians have stood their ground
since slacker days of scrub and brackens,
when this last house at Grassrigg was the seven stirks' barn.

Between us and the north steadies the mother
of them all, thick-waisted, wide as she's tall,
lengthy innumerable arms extended
in the carer's cantilever,
to reach wall, slope, sheep tugging
at her fingers, sustain
a hundred hungering insect species, tray
a thousand eggcups
to feed the hoodlum squirrel, the flashy jay.

And well away among grasses
the hidden hoard hatches;
inklings wake
up; three gold tongues quirk.

August

Sorbus aucuparia

I'm most at home on the airy fell,
feet among heather and bilberry,
where pipits flit to my gleaming limbs
streaming into the sky.

Or clinging by a toe-hold
in the ravine wall, a rock gymnast,
thrilling to the spumy torrent's fume,
a dipper on my wrist.

Here in the wood I'm overshadowed
by the voluminous green baize gowns
of August matrons' middle-aged spread.
Slight, spinsterly, aloof

from the tossing gossip –
'Shocking wind! Call this summer?' –
jostling on over my head,
I lean, long

towards the open,
where I could be solitary,
stand poised in a glory
of silver skin and coral costume jewellery.

Bonny as a bush of bright apples,
lush as a jungle of oranges,
carnival as a tower
of runner beans in flower,

I'd set my cap
at every smart cock blackbird,
and with the hens
play lipstick lesbian.

Scarlet harlot, berry tart,
free of stifling umbrage I'd part
glossy lips to sing, flash ringed fingers,
dare at last to have my fling.

September

Sambucus nigra

In June I put on an apron and eau de Cologne,
hand round cleanly pancheons,
sprays Wensleydale-meadowsweet-cream,
to scald, steep,
and store, muscat-sweet.

Now my boons are darker:
dishes of caviar;
blackberry lobes exploded,
re-assembled on an umbel; fieldmice eyes;
currants for a flock of fairy flies.

And I've grown like billy-o,
cuttlefish roots swarming among stones,
suckering clay,
mud-mouthing 'Grow, grow'
from depths below

to shoots tentacling the thicket.
Bark grizzle, warted, corky,
rind hard as box, pith pap-soft,
hollow-bore stems pipe
my life between wet and light.

Now leaves drain pale.
Sanguine capillaries
swell bloody pustules
on the vampire chandeliers,
sachets of gore to gorge the farewell wheatears.

I survive middens and graveyards,
thrive alongside the yellow-fanged nettle
in the shanty town ruins of elms,
know how to ward off bluebottle,
witch, and Devil.

Younger than I seem, older than my age,
I will not live long, yet they call me a sage.

Pinus sylvestris

I stand high on a hill by the road.
My head is slate stratus cloud
rafted above rufous branches

lifting to signal. What I know
makes my bark bleed. Some say I mark
where armies' shock rusted the grass.

Or where drovers with trampling bullocks
lodged on their way south to the marts,
with news of far straths and glens,

Feshie or Affric, hemmed
by four-thousand-foot Cairngorms or rocky Beinns,
where once with birch and heather

I lived in my native land
before sheep ate its people and trees.
Now here in the green of small fells and soft dales I stand.

October

Prunus spinosa

You produce incrustations of grapes, bloomy black;
when I nibble a little at one of them,
it bites back.

You stretch out a branch to save me when I slip;
slide an inch of needle into my palm,
and rip.

I set you out as a hedgerow to guard my land;
you turn and march multiplied in on me, bayonets fixed,
brigand band.

Yet, when winter holds on fast, and spring comes slow,
you sprinkle your black thorns with flowers,
outfacing snow.

Malus sylvestris

See that little thicket tree
with flesh-pink blossom
hidden deep in the wood,
yet familiar, human,
as bread or blood?

So like my orchard: modern 'Discovery',
'Ashmead's Kernel' from the eighteenth century,
and 'Court Pendu Plat'
the Romans brought over.
But it's much older than that.

Or the feral giant in the outgrown field hedge
flowering freely,
occasional green glut
picked at only by blackbirds;
but wilder than that.

Aboriginal of this land,
a supplanted race,
still seeded here and there in waste
wood places, or along the Roudsea strand,
where little else can stand the saltwind's pace.

Twigged thickly, spurred and spined,
do you hold, in rings or rind
the memory we have in common?
how your gold tart fruit was gathered,
roasted on the fire,
by stone age woman.

November

Taxus baccata

I brood the tombstones like a mother bird
sitting out centuries of sun and rain;
I'd grown here long before this church and yard
were built in my wild sanctuary to contain
my trunk's congealed muscle, marbled meat,
a rock-hard living carcass cradling bones;
my cherry-pink arils, thrushes' berry sweets,
bright cups for bitter nuts, their toxic stones;

flat-fingered needles, deepest of all greens,
potent with poison to excise and probe
cancers from those poor short-lived human weeds
recently seeded all over the globe,
whose red sap flows and flushes much too fast
through softwood flesh, not dense enough to last.

Corylus avellana

The woods are going grey now;
except, here and there,
the ginger moustaches of larches,
beeches' flaming hair.

And mottled limes and lemons
dappled through the understorey
on these most dogged of trees;
the pawns, the infantry,

the spear-carriers,
the peasantry,
thick on the ground
in every common wood in the country.

Good neighbours,
willing to lend
from their stands, bronze rods
and sinewy wands

for our beansticks, broomsticks,
hedge-stakes and hurdles,
thatchers' spars and liggers,
cottage-wall wattles.

Each leaf-shucked wooden shell
cradles a cranium seed
milky white as a miniature coconut,
drying dense and sweet

as a silver nutmeg
and a golden pear
bringing the chiselling squirrel
and the King of Spain's daughter

to join us all on Nutcrack Night
when everyone gets cracking,
and teeth are broke on brazen cobs
and po-faced priests sent packing.

And when most folk have turned in
now it's back-end,
and they're waving cheery goodbyes
with round yellow hands,

on the quiet, meanwhile,
they're hatching romance:
tiny fingers twiddle
in a sprightly catkin dance;

soon to flail on whippy twigs
through wintry gales' blast,
dangle gloveless
in biting frost.

And all to be first
when the crimson mouths open,
when the lambs' tails are jiggling,
to walk out with the brown-eyed maiden
up and down the spring copse

Ilex aquifolium

Well, that's over again. They put it on
every year, you know. All sorts of drama.
Do a lot of shouting, waving their arms about.
Dress up garish, act like prima donnas.
Finale, some of them strip right off,
rest hang about in rags, bloodshot,
gasping out the last few leaf drops.
Must take it out of you.

Us? Oh, pretty much the same as usual, thanks.
Been here on this old field-bank
at the edge of Cowby Wood for as long
as we can remember, haven't we, dear?
Tall new neighbours, of course, overlooking,
but they don't give us much bother.
We get a lot done
before they even wake up in the spring.

We were a handsome pair.
Two plump pyramids spiring up.
Always a bit leathery, of course, bit prickly,
not like some of your sensitive souls
that get browsed out, or shrivel up
as soon as the weather turns colder.
But good and glossy,
it's a healthy outdoor life.

And just look at my wife!
Getting ready for the party.
Yes, we've both taken a few knocks,
stumpier than we were,
the odd bump and bulge, bunion and knot.
But when she's done herself up,
no one can touch her! Her bosom's
all laden with berries, right up to the chin!

None of the young ones could put on a spread
like that, never missing a year.
Does my old heartwood good. Christmas tree?
She's the real thing. Brights the whole winter up
with her cheery flush. Last me a lifetime.
See, it's our ruby wedding.
My shiny dark beauty, my buxom old bride,
bolt upright beside me, in all that white.

Mrs *Ilex aquifolium*

Don't listen to a word he says. Old softie.
Makes me sound like a fashion plate. Too busy!
Children, grandchildren. Woods full of them,
up and running, sharp as anything.
Have to smile, the little girls
in their first party berries. Bright as buttons.
Ilex and me, started a dynasty, no mistake.
Now, if you'll excuse me. Got to ice my cake.

Postscript

Ulmus procera

I am the grey form.
I am the bone one.
Plague came,
and all my kind were done.

Boreholes riddle me,
patches of skin still cling.
Woodpeckers, lice and titmice
have found their way in.

Do not cut me down.
Do not clear me away.
Among all the greenery
I am your memento mori.
I stay.

Answers

Crataegus monogyna p.45
Hawthorn is also known as May or Quickthorn, and there is an abundance of folk names for its berries. Tough and spiny, it is universally used for hedging and as a boundary marker. Hawthorn leaves are the first to open in early spring, and are sometimes represented in the Green Man's beard. The May Queen festivities were associated with lovemaking outside in the woods, and there is a widespread belief that if the blossom is brought indoors, the mother of the house will die.

Betula pendula p.47
Silver Birch was one of the first trees to return to Britain after the last Ice Age and survives further north than any other. A pioneer species, quickly seeding into waste ground on acid soils, it is often regarded as a weed. Yet it is valuable to birds and graceful at all times of year. In winter, when the small leaves have yellowed and fallen, a purple-black mesh of twigs shows above white or soft pink bark marked with fine horizontal lines and deep vertical cracks.

Alnus glutinosa p.51
Alder thrives in damp places. In late winter the twigs are crowded with last year's empty seed 'cones', as well as tiny new female 'berries' and male catkins which droop and turn crimson as they develop. The leaves open late and are slightly sticky or 'glutinous', hence the name. They stay dark green on the branches till early winter. Alder wood is said to 'bleed' because it stains reddish when cut.

Salix caprea p.52
Goat Willow, also known as Pussy Willow, stands out in early spring when its flowers open on bare twigs. Male trees bear the distinctive short catkins or 'pussies', silky grey at first, then turning golden yellow with pollen.

Acer pseudoplatanus p.55
Sycamore was introduced into Britain from central Europe, possibly as early as the 15th century. Fully naturalised, it seeds prolifically, and is not always welcome, though it can grow into a massive rugged tree which thrives even in the most exposed places. The yellow-green tassels of flowers burst from pink sepals, and the young leaves have a rosy tinge. Later in the year they drip with aphid secretions, are blackened by tar-spot fungus, and fall early to form a slimy blanket.

Larix decidua p.56
Larch was introduced into Britain from Alpine regions in the 17th century, and is planted as a shelter belt and for timber. It is unusual in being a deciduous conifer. Its graceful upswept branches put on fresh green needles in spring which turn orange before falling in autumn. The tiny red tufts of female flowers, carried upright on the twigs, grow into small cones.

Ulmus glabra p.58

Wych Elm is the native elm of northern Britain, preferring moist conditions, and often seen in hedgerows and on riverbanks. 'Wych' indicates pliancy, and indeed its arching branches and long leaves give it an almost weeping appearance. In early spring the naked twigs, which grow in the 'fishbone' formation characteristic of elm, carry rosettes of pale green seed capsules. Young trees flourish, but, as they mature, most succumb to Dutch elm disease, like their cousins the English elms (see *Ulmus procera*).

Fraxinus excelsior p.63

Ash is the last tree to put on leaves, sometimes not until June in the north, and it is the first to shed them in October. Its shoots droop and then curl upwards, 'bouncing' in the wind. The bunched keys turn brown and may hang on the tree all winter. Flowers are produced in tufts, the male ones purple, the female green. Some single-sex trees change gender every year, some carry individual branches of the opposite sex, some regularly carry both male and female flowers, and some produce dual-sex ('perfect') flowers. Ash is especially common on alkaline soils, and will grow out of limestone pavements and outcrops.

Prunus avium p.64

Wild Cherry or Gean grows wild on woodland margins. It stands out in spring when it bears white blossom before the leaves are fully open, and again in autumn when its foliage can turn a rich red. Often planted in parks and gardens, it is a larger tree than any of the non-native ornamental cherries. The Latin name '*avium*' means 'of birds', and in late summer the small dark red fruits attract blackbirds and thrushes.

Prunus padus p.64

Bird Cherry (not to be confused with *Prunus avium*) is a small tree or large shrub, found in hedgerows in northern Britain, where it has many local names. Its small smooth oval leaves, of a warm green, appear at the same time as the racemes of fragrant cream-coloured flowers, which eventually droop rather like lilac, and produce strings of bitter black fruits. The caterpillar larvae of the ermine moth sometimes weave vast communal webs over whole hedges of bird cherry, which are then completely defoliated.

Fagus sylvatica p.67

Beech is probably native only to southern Britain, though planted populations in the north are now seeding freely. It is one of our tallest trees, but its shallow root-plate makes it particularly susceptible to being blown over by strong winds. Its fine smooth bark and lengthy undulating branches are unmistakable. In spring the translucent leaves glow a brilliant green; in autumn they blaze.

Quercus petraea x robur p.69
Sessile Oak (*Quercus petraea*) is a tree of northern wildwood, thriving on stony ground. Its stalkless acorns, which sit directly on the twigs, distinguish it from **English Oak** (*Quercus robur*). However, many northern trees are hybrids, a result of extensive planting of English Oak. Oaks support more insect species than any other tree. The acorns are plucked by jays and buried in open ground away from the parent tree, where they may germinate and grow on as oaklings. The more intensive grazing of the late 20th century halted such tree regeneration in many wood pastures.

Sorbus aucuparia p.73
Rowan or Mountain Ash (no relation to the true ash, though it has similarly pinnate leaves) is a small tree of acid soils, preferring open ground and rocky places in the north. Its cleanly ascending branches stay smooth and silvery as the tree ages. The flat heads of cream flowers open in late spring, and by late summer it carries bright scarlet fruits which are quickly eaten by birds.

Sambucus nigra p.75
Elder, also known as Boontree, Boortree, or Fairy Tree, was believed to have magic power to ward off evil. Its malodorous branches protected cattle from flies, and its stems, hollowed of their pith, were used as bellows-pipes. Elderflower cordial is still made from the fragrant flowers. Favouring rich soils, it flourishes in rubbish tips and graveyards. Though short-lived, it is vigorous; its fleshy white roots spread quickly through heavy soil and its arching branches push up through undergrowth. Elderberries are especially valuable to migrant birds, as they contain an enzyme which helps convert sugars into body fat to fuel the long journey.

Pinus sylvestris p.76
Scots Pine, a native of northern Britain, was the keystone tree of the Old Caledonian Forest which extended across the Scottish Highlands. Though largely destroyed by felling and overgrazing, remnants survive, for example in Glen Affric (Wester Ross) and Glen Feshie (Cairngorms). Stands of pine on English hills are said to mark the sites of old battles, or, more likely, to have been planted as waymarks by Highland drovers. As the tree ages, lower branches tend to fall, leaving flattened masses of dark foliage at the top. The reddish scaly bark sometimes exudes resin.

Prunus spinosa p.79
Sloe or Blackthorn is probably an ancestor of the plum (*Prunus domestica*), yet its small blue-black fruits are intensely sour. Its long and vicious spines make it an effective alternative to hawthorn as a hedging plant, and it will sucker to form dense thickets. Borne on bare branches before the leaves open, its white flowers are usually the first wild blossom of spring.

Malus sylvestris p.80
Crab-apple is now a rather scarce small tree of old woods and hedges. It is quite distinct from the thousands of varieties of Orchard Apple (*Malus domestica*), which were bred from central Asian stock, and often seed as 'wildlings' – apple trees of unknown provenance growing wild by roads or in hedgerows. The true native Crab is distinguishable from these by its tousled form, densely twiggy branches, and smaller, oval, glossy leaves, lacking fine hairs on the underside. It is remarkably hardy.

Taxus baccata p.85
Yew can live for thousands of years, perhaps forever, because of its capacity to regenerate from outer wood. Perhaps for this reason prehistoric people seem to have chosen yew groves for their sacred sites and burial mounds. Christian churches were later built in these places, and many ancient yews were incorporated into graveyards. Yew is poisonous in all its parts, except for the red flesh of the arils or fruits which are eaten by birds. In recent years, the alkaloids in yew bark and leaves have proved effective in treating cancers.

Corylus avellana p.86
Hazel, with its multi-stemmed habit and straight branches, has traditionally been managed by coppicing; the stems are cut to the ground on a regular rotation to stimulate regrowth of pliable young wands for woodcraft. Stored nuts were brought out in

November, and sometimes cracked in church!
The nursery rhyme 'I had a little nut-tree', and the folksong 'The nut-brown maiden', may refer to hazel. Trees carry their male catkins through the winter; in spring these 'lambs' tails' open to pollinate the tiny red female flowers.

Ilex aquifolium p.89
Holly is our most common evergreen. Tolerant of shading by taller trees, it is currently seeding profusely in woodland understorey. Its habit is spire-shaped and upright, the grey bark often roughened and warted. The glossy leaves are heavily spined on young plants, and on the lower branches of mature ones, to deter browsing animals. Male and female trees are distinct; only the female bears berries. The ancient custom of bringing berried holly branches into the house at midwinter originated long before the 19th century introduction of the fir 'Christmas tree'.

Ulmus procera p.91
English Elm was a lofty tree commonly seen in the fields of southern England, and also planted in the north. In the late 1960s Dutch elm disease, a lethal fungus spread by bark-beetles, worked its way up the country, killing most of the population. The dead elms stood for many years, eerily echoing their age-old reputation as reminders of mortality. Most have now been felled (though suckers are rising, phoenix-like, from the roots).

Part Three
Family Tree

Bramley's Seedling

Dad says, the front window is different,
and the road behind us fast and loud
where then there were dray-horses hauling.

Down the side, the strip where
his mother grew marigolds. Behind, the bathroom
his father built on, though the shed

he'd helped him build is gone.
Asphalt obscures the narrow plot
they'd made the most of.

He sees through it: rows of raspberries, spuds, the seat
the old man had made for his Mary
to rest from her work in the house,

gracing him as he dug;
she never stopped working.
Down the end, Dad remembers,

were a pair of apples his parents planted.
And I go to them:
huge, neglected, stalwart, still here

in this scruffy patch of grass.
Survived seventy years.
I greet rough bark,

pick up a windfall, small, green,
pocket it, take in what I can
of their stoic and honourable time.

Holm Oak

'All that was the garden', says my cousin, 'of Forty-nine'.
The mansion our Grandpa, taken root from the Continent,
bought when he'd made his fortune.
Dedicated to the wife he worshipped, 'Dulcieholme'.
Twenty new houses grow out of blank concrete. No sign
of our grandparents' place and time.

Looking back I notice the pavement is shadowed
by a dark holm oak. Grave grey bark
distinguished as a pinstripe City suit.
Leaves leathery as a cigar, evergreen and sharp,
rolled inward to endure drought.
Quercus ilex from the south, holding its own

amongst gold of English oaks on this Croydon road.
'Chêne vert', that densely shades its native
Côte d'Azure. And I'm suddenly sure
our grandfather planted it here,
to commemorate strolls on the front at Beauvallon,
his darling, his 'Dulcette', still on his arm.

May Day Dream

'Though he walked the road to London
to find work, your grandfather was always
a countryman at heart'. Arthur Day.
Our name may have meant 'Dairyman'.

I see a man rising in the dark
to milk balloon-uddered cows,
urge them out at dawn
into moon-daisy meadows.

Now I drive back into a dale
brimming with cream. Home.
May's great curds floating
across fields. Bowls of it on rowans.

Cow parsley bubbling up. Butter
cups. And our lane, newly asphalted,
leads to my converted barn,
splashed with milk-white flowers
round the byre, beasts long gone.

Oaks

Down in Sussex the great oaks are turning gold,
roaring shaggy-layered manes,
or burnishing in low sun,
might of muscled limbs quiet.
Their heavy brocaded branches, high
as Chichester cathedral bell-tower, sway
above the cottage up Buddington Lane.

It's been nearly half a century.
Long enough, maybe, for them to have noticed
the goings-on far below: matchbox house extension,
orchard tufting up, mustard-and-cress of a garden.
And how the little creatures liked to creep
and sit between their huge gnarled paws,
trusting them, dropping off to sleep.

Tools

I've already brought back his billhook.
Sliced the branches cleanly
off the sycamore poles from the pollard
at the top of the meadow.
Chucked them over the fence for my neighbours' kindling,
leaving myself a slew of
smooth trunks to saw up for the winter.
Satisfying.

Going to get his splitting-axe as well --
it's lying on the guest-room floor waiting
for the removal van,
huge Green-Knight head
resting on the boards,
curved hickory shaft
curled asleep at last.
(Can I really swing that?).

But the chain-saw.
Sitting on the larder shelf
between tins of anchovies
and out-of-date tomato soup.
I've been thinking maybe I should get one
sometime, when I'm not so scared of it
slicing my fingers off, or
savaging my leg like a mad dog.

Thing is I'm not that keen on more mechanical gadgets, not green.
Anyway I like hand-sawing. The slowness. It's a kind of meditation,
counting the strokes – PUSH-pull PUSH-pull – going into scores,
took 500 to get through that bird cherry chunk Paul Postlethwaite left
when he laid the old hedge at the edge of the wood.
I didn't mind.
Low sun on my face, keeping warm, what could be better?

But if I'm really seriously trying
to heat the house with wood? Not just playing?
O.K., so I'm steadily slogging through that stack of old fence-posts,
7 or 8 at a time, bit by bit
adding to the stock in the shed.
But there's a whole furnace-full up the hill,
dinosaur spines,
a mammoth multi-trunk sycamore
just crying out to be coppiced.
Can't kid myself I'd take the frame to them.

Do you know, says Emma,
I think you should get a new one?
If you want one. With a safety cut-out?

Dad didn't have that.
Were his legs leather, then,
his fingers iron?

Pollen

Sulphur dust on the dashboard; a fine
deposit, acid yellow as a fifties design.
I'd stopped the car by a copse, broken off
hazel twigs jittering charged-up catkins.
Back at the house, I'd balanced them,
Japanese, in a thick glass vase
for Dad's room, to remind him
all was not lost, spring was coming.

They gave him hayfever, were banished,
then thrown out. Emptied tassels tarnished.
Still on the dashboard the traces
of gold dust.   Like
your rings gloves scarves scent glasses,
your Earl Grey tea-bags, Marmite, teeth, toothbrushes,
and, framed, on every surface, your old faces.
Your things, your sheddings, your signs of life. Your graces.

Levin Down: after the hospital visit

No time more precious than this;
veined dogwood's ruby bleed,
whitebeam's ashen glance,
as goldfinches dance up and away
from fat berries' opulence.

Spindles dispense pink capsules,
sharp juniper,
bitter sloe, bloomy blue,
while tiny poison lanterns hang
in the healing darkness of yew.

The ground is a tissue of finery
stitched from cut-leaved
cranesbill, burnet, silverweed,
with clustered bell-flower's amethyst phials,
wild marjoram richly ragged with seed.

And the sun is warmly attentive
alike to jet beads of purging buckthorn,
and rabbits' scattered largesse;
red garlands of bryony, and rose nylon twine
necklacing the hedge;

the flint, diamond edge shrouded in this chalk-bed
laid down by oceans' billions dead,
and the relic sheep's shin,
ivory knuckle still half-sheathed
in its antique carpet of skin.

Christmas Tree in Andalucia

I'm missing a small northern spruce in the house
like the one we hung with the fragile
family silver balls that last time. Now

in this strange land I must find my own.
Marvel at the orchards' green darknesses baubled
bright with orange suns and lemon moons.

Celebrate with persimmons, luminous as light bulbs
strung along bare branches; pomegranates
cracking open their gift boxes of rosy gems.

Give thanks, not for a partridge in a pear tree, but,
among white-berried sprays
of Persian lilac, a collared dove

perched alone. And rejoice
that everywhere, far across the mountainsides,
grey-haired olives, the enduring inhabitants,

are ripening, for the thousandth time,
their New Year's staple and sustaining crop.

Figs

There were huge pancheons
I could haul myself upright and hold onto.
Red clay outside, lip and all within
glazed a rich yellow-cream,
open wide to the London
terrace-garden heat.

They held my mother's figs, whose curling grey trunks,
peculiar as elephants' at the Zoo,
protruded small green knobs, that never
seemed to ripen. It was the leaves she loved,
the broad bold palms, sandpaper to the touch,
raised to enfold or applaud,

and invoke the Mediterranean:
first holidays on the continent
after the war, Adam and Eve's return
to sunbathe in Eden. Like the savour
of ratatouille and bouquet garni
once rationing was over.

With pots of vermilion geraniums, flags of gaiety
she hung out on the trellis, and forever
had to water. Till fifty years later
when she couldn't any more.
Out of cracked dustbowls
stick the crooked ghosts.

And now, to find her great green hands,
I have to go home. Here they are, lifting
from my carefully-trained fans,
content enough to droop
deepening bags of fruit,
on the tall stone wall, facing
a cool northern sun.

Paula Day was born in London, the daughter of
designers Robin and Lucienne Day. After reading
English at Cambridge she moved to Cumbria,
and completed a Ph.D thesis on nature imagery in
women's poetry. For many years she ran pioneering
outdoors holidays for women from her hillside home
in the Lune Valley, between the Lake District and
the Yorkshire Dales. As well as writing, she designs
gardens, and, as Chair of The Robin and Lucienne Day
Foundation, she currently divides her time between
Cumbria and Chichester, West Sussex.

Val Corbett is a freelance photographer, based in the Lowther Valley on the eastern fringes of the Lake District. Over the past twenty-five years she has built up an extensive photographic library of Cumbria (www.valcorbettphotography.com). Her photographs of gardens appear regularly in national magazines such as *Country Life*. Her own recent books include *Winter in the Lake District* and *Rainy Days in the Lake District*, and she collaborated on *Gardens of the Lake District* and *Jack's Yak*, both of which won the 'Lakeland Book of the Year' award.